Super Kitty

Author: **Mary Anne Sheehan**
and **Special Guest**

AuthorHouse™
1663 Liberty Drive
Bloomington, IN 47403
www.authorhouse.com
Phone: 833-262-8899

Because of the dynamic nature of the Internet, any web addresses or links contained in this book may have changed since publication and may no longer be valid. The views expressed in this work are solely those of the author and do not necessarily reflect the views of the publisher, and the publisher hereby disclaims any responsibility for them.

Any people depicted in stock imagery provided by Getty Images are models, and such images are being used for illustrative purposes only. Certain stock imagery © Getty Images.

This book is printed on acid-free paper.

ISBN: 978-1-6655-4152-7 (sc)
        978-1-6655-4153-4 (e)

Print information available on the last page.

Published by AuthorHouse 10/21/2021

authorHOUSE®

Dedication

This book is dedicated to all the generous people who have opened their homes and enriched their lives by adopting a pet. It is dedicated to the rescue cats, who through no fault of their own, wind up on the street and are taken in at rescue centers. These cats wait patiently to find loving homes and deserve to be protected and loved. This book is also dedicated to my previous cat, Spankie, who lived to 20 and passed on in 2020. I knew it was time to for me to open my heart and adopt again. When I spotted the sweet calico kitten the day I visited the Caffeinated Cat (CC) rescue center, she was a sight for sore eyes! From the moment I signed the adoption papers and held my little bundle of joy, I have loved spending every minute with her. She is a smart and loving cat who provides me hours of fun, enjoyment and companionship.

When you finish reading this book, please make a donation to the Caffeinated Cat (CC). Your donation will allow more rescue cats to be adopted into loving homes. If you cannot donate money, consider gifting your time and visiting a rescue center near you. They are always in need of cat litter, toys, and every donation helps more cats as await their forever homes.

Did you know?

- According to the Human Society, the estimated number of cats in the US is between 30 to 40 million?

- Only 2% of those cats are spayed

- 80% of new kittens are from stray, abandoned or feral cats

- 70% of cats are euthanized in shelters!

- No matter where you live, rescue cats are in need of homes

- To find a cat to adopt, go to:

https:cat.rescueme.org

Chapter Index

CHAPTER 1:

Super Kitty finds a home

After recently moving to Florida, I was ready for a new companion, but the pet store I visited had no pets available for adoption. Instead, they referred me to the Caffeinated Cat (CC), a 501C3, in Jacksonville Beach that takes in rescue cats.

When I walked into the CC, I ordered coffee and admired the children's artwork that decorates the walls. I met the owner and then mingled with several rescue cats (12 to be exact) in a large cozy sunroom surrounded by full length windows on three walls. I spotted Super Kitty who, at the time, was sleeping in a wicker basket and laying on ribbons and toys. I sat down and gently picked up the tiny white, black and orange kitty and held her for the very first time.

Although this kitten kept her eyes shut the entire time I held her close to my chest she purred loudly. I could tell she was a loving Calico cat despite being just over two months old. She had been found on the street and taken to the CC. Since her arrival there, she was spayed and chipped, so in case she ever gets lost, she can be returned to her owner. In addition, her left ear was clipped to indicate that she was spayed and cannot have kittens.

Calico: *most calico cats are female, and the typical calico has large patches of white with similar patches of black and orange. Calico cats cannot be bred, and calico cats are the official cat of the state of California.*

I immediately asked about adopting this Super Kitty, and she was available! I filled out the adoption paperwork on the spot and paid a small fee. I wanted to give this adorable cat a good home, and since I had just moved into a new apartment, I would need time to create a safe and comfortable home for her. First I purchased a cozy hanging bed, a big bag of dry kitten food, cans of wet kitten food, toys, and litter. One week later, I was headed back to the CC to pick up Super Kitty and take her home where she would be loved and cared for many years to come.

Now all that was needed is a new name. I invited friends on Facebook to suggest names for my new bundle of joy. I received over 70 suggestions, but I felt they didn't quite capture Super Kitty's personality. A few of the names included: Bella, Domino, and Flo, but as I drove home with Super Kitty laying quietly in her carrier on the back seat – never once did she meow. I didn't have to rush to name her. I had time to think about what to name her and in fact, she was alert and watched my every move. I knew her name would come to me as we got to know each other better.

Super Kitty spent her first few days hiding in her new home. She spent a lot of her time under the counter sandwiched between the stove and cabinet. When she was coaxed out from underneath the counter, she would tentatively exit and, of course, begin sniffing every inch of the five rooms in the apartment. As Super Kitty grew more comfortable in her new home and surroundings, she was more relaxed. She would jump up onto my lap wanting attention and purr until I petted and cuddled her, usually while I was typing on my laptop. So I knew she was a keeper!

The day I adopted Ginger

Super Kitty's Point of View

It was just another day at the Caffeinated Cat (CC), and I was trying to position myself in a sunny place so I could take my afternoon nap where no other cat could find me. I was perched up high in a dresser drawer on the south facing wall with a soft blanket that doubles as my bed, and it is out of sight of the other cats. I needed to catch up on my sleep as I was exhausted from the night before because the other cats were running around and kept me from sleeping. I guess it is what cats do!

I was just dozing off to sleep when I felt the all too familiar hands around me. That human came back and you guessed it – it was during my *cat nap*! Yet again, she picked me up just as I began purring. I was so tired, I couldn't open my heavy eyes. My *cat nap* was interrupted for the fifth time today which was typical because humans don't care if they wake you up from your nap! The CC allows humans to come into our sunroom between the hours of 12 to 6 p.m.

<u>*Cat Nap*</u>: *a very short light nap*

Anyway, I thought this human had a nice low voice and she spoke softly to me. She picked me up, scratched my chin and the top of my head which I absolutely love because it helps me fall asleep! In fact, I thought she was a good petter, and before I knew it, I nodded off to sleep again but this time in her arms.

When I woke up and opened my eyes wide and yawned and stretched, she quickly picked me up and placed me in a black carrier with a screen. Together we left the CC and for the very first time, I was outside the sunroom. The first thing I could smell was the fresh damp salt air, and there was so much to see! I kept my eyes wide open and noticed that my heart was beating faster and pounding with excitement. I saw fluffy white cloud formations in the sky that looked like giant cotton balls, and the temperature was much cooler than it was in the sunroom that I called home. I couldn't remember the last time I smelled fresh air and saw the trees moving in the wind against the skyline.

A few minutes later, I was finally in the car when I heard a loud sound and watched as she rolled down the windows. I took in the smells and sights of the outdoors as the car began moving. I saw tall green trees with fan like leaves at the very top blowing back and forth along both sides of the road. I watched small black and white birds dart across the skyline that was filling up with big gray clouds. There were many different colored cars and people walking and riding bicycles in all directions. It was a lot for my eyes to take in. Frankly, there was so much to look at that I didn't have time to meow during my first car ride ever. A few minutes later, the car pulled into a parking lot outside a beige two story building and stopped. She got out and picked up my carrier and together we went inside.

When we exited the car, my heart was beating fast and almost stopped because I wasn't sure what to expect. We went inside and she closed a blue door behind us. I kept myself very still when she placed the carrier on the brown floor. She bent down and spoke softly to me while unzipping the top of the carrier. She picked me up to reassure me everything would be okay. My heartbeat began to slow down a little bit and she placed me on the rug in front of the fireplace. However, I kept my body close to the ground not knowing what to expect in my new surroundings.

Wow, this place was huge! I sniffed the air in every room, and I didn't smell any other cats. I could begin investigating because you never know when you may need a quick exit or a good hiding spot. The first thing I found was a bowl filled with crunchy dry food and water for me. At that moment, I realized I would no longer have to share food with other cats. I continued my exploration sniffing the two bathrooms and the two bedrooms and basically every corner of the entire apartment. After I did that, I ate every morsel of food in the bowl, and now I was ready to settle in for my first cat nap in my new residence.

I found a great little hiding spot in the kitchen on the floor where there was an opening between the stove and the cabinet where no one could reach me. After a few hours of sleep, I heard someone's voice calling awakening me. I began my ritual of stretching and yawning, and then I remembered I was no longer at the CC, so I slowly left my hiding spot and walked curiously toward the voice that was calling me.

Surprise, surprise – my owner was waiting for me and presented me with a bowl of wet food that she had warmed up in the microwave. She put it down, and I devoured every morsel because I never tasted wet food before - all I ever had was dry food. I thought to myself: this new home and owner might just work out after all.

CHAPTER 2:

Super Kitty's name

Super Kitty was just a little shy of three months when she was introduced to her new home. After just a few days, coaxing her to come out from her hiding spot was no longer necessary. I noticed she quickly became more comfortable in her new surroundings and preferred sleeping on the couch or on one of the two big beds. After a week or so, she was hiding less, eating more, and just loved exploring her new home.

Super Kitty quickly figured out her feeding schedule which dictates her sleep schedule. In the morning she performs her ritualistic happy dance outside my bedroom door. After I wake up each morning, I greet her and I make my coffee, but first I prepare her breakfast before my own. Her bowl consists of warmed wet food buried under dry crunchy kitten food. After she finishes eating every morsel, she hops up on my lap to say thank you and purrs herself to sleep <u>on my chest.</u>

As I continued to think about what to name her, I made a post on FB asking for friends' suggestions. Some of the suggested names were cute, but did not quite capture my kitten's spirit. I wanted her name to reflect her curiosity, affection and intellect. After a few days of deliberation, I decided to name her Ginger. This name suited her big patches of orange and black against her white fur background. She was still a kitten that thought I was her mother as she needed to be held and cuddled. So it seems Ginger and Mary Anne were going to be spending a lot of quality time together for many years to come!

Super Kitty's perspective:

In my short life I have been called a lot of names, some of which I didn't answer to. I know my owner cares about me because she feeds me regularly, holds me close, combs my fur, pets me all the time, and gives me treats! I have an entire cabinet that holds all my treats, and a basket to hold my cat nip and toys! I even have my own hanging bed in the second bedroom, but honestly, I prefer sleeping on her lap or on one of the big beds.

So if she wants to call me Ginger, I am okay with that! Just keep the toys, treats and food coming! My favorite new habit is to wake up early and wait outside her bedroom door until she opens it. Some days I have to wait a very long time, but at that point, I am so excited that I begin my happy dance and meow to communicate my hunger. Together we go into the kitchen where she prepares my breakfast while I dance between her feet and impatiently meow because I am so hungry.

When she finally presents me with my bowl of food and fresh water and ice, I devour all of it - no surprise there! After breakfast she combs my fur and gives me treats. <u>Okay full disclosure</u>: the truth is she gives me treats to distract me so she can trim my claws which are growing fast and because I have been climbing up her red leather chair and scratching the new brown couch.

Since I'm a kitten, I am teething and scratching everything in sight, and I know she is not happy with me climbing up the back of her favorite reading chair - the red leather one and the brown couch. Hey, I can't help scratching, it is what kittens do. I don't always cooperate when she tries to trim my nails, and I need to do better and stop scratching and biting everything. To be perfectly honest, I am enjoying my new home, my new name, and I love my owner!

CHAPTER 3:

Super Kitty's First Field Trip:

Three weeks after bringing Ginger home, it was time for her first veterinarian appointment for a required vaccine. When we arrived at the veterinarian office, we were advised to wait in the car outside the office building due to covid, and wait until an exam room was disinfected and became available. I was worried about how Ginger would react, but she was relaxed and curious and waited patiently in the back seat. When it was time to go in, she was a big hit with the staff. It seems, everyone who comes in contact with her, cannot keep their hands off her, and this includes the veterinarian!

Veterinarian appointment

When we entered the room, Ginger immediately jumped down off the examination table to explore everything in sight. First, she looked the pictures on the wall, played with the scale, jumped into the sink and, of course, easily located the treat jar. The veterinarian walked in and greeted both of us. He began examining Ginger and said, "She's in perfect shape" and proceeded to open the treat jar which immediately caught Ginger's attention. He took her temperature and both the technician and the veterinarian held her while giving her a treat to distract her from the sting of the needle and her first shot. I asked questions regarding her health, and I was advised there were no concerns.

Ginger was all set to go until her next shot appointment. Kittens, just like children, need vaccinations when they are young. Ginger appeared to enjoy her visit to the veterinarian, and she was not shy at all. She let everyone pet her and she complied with all their requests without meowing. It was clear that everyone enjoyed meeting her the first time. I did inquire about declawing her, and I was advised to wait until she was six months before doing so. I researched laser surgery and discovered it can be very painful. I decided I will look into alternatives because Ginger is perfect the way she is!

Ginger's point of view:

I love going for car rides, and I got to take another one today. I noticed my owner put some treats into a small plastic bag, so I was trying to be good so she would give me some. I jumped right into my carrier and waited until she zipped it up and placed me on the back seat. It was a hotter day than the last time we took a car ride so the windows were rolled down. As we travelled down a busy street to our destination, I was enjoying the sights and sounds of the city coming in through the car windows.

We traveled fast and passed many cars, stores, and people before turning into a parking lot outside a big white building. Someone came to the car window with a clip board and asked some questions. My owner answered the questions and we waited in the car until it was our turn to go inside. I got a treat just for sitting quietly. A cat could get used to this!

My owner's phone rang notifying her it was time for us to go inside for my appointment. I was excited, and immediately I smelled disinfectant and the scent of other animals as we entered the building. They put us in a very small room, but there was a lot for me to explore, and I had a hunch there would be treats somewhere. A technician came in to weigh me and put me on a scale. It registered 3.4 pounds. Because I sat still, I got a treat! Next the veterinarian came in and spoke while he poked and prodded my stomach and rib cage. A minute later he scratched my head and at the same time gave me a shot. I was focused on the treats which distracted me. All in all, I really enjoyed my first field trip. I wondered to myself, "When would we be going on another field trip?"

CHAPTER 4:

Daily Routine

When we arrived home from the appointment, Ginger was exhausted and hid underneath the bed. She ate her food but vomited a short time later and slept most of the day. I guess the shot was too much for her small body to handle, and it wore her out. I tried to feed her a few treats, but it was clear that Ginger wanted to be left alone. I periodically checked in on her, but she was not interacting with me. By the next morning she was feeling better and was back to her feisty ways.

She awoke me with her meowing to indicate her hunger and impatience with me for taking time to get up and make my bed and fix my coffee first. I fixed her favorite and biggest meal of the day: breakfast. Ginger attacked the food with her ravenous kitten appetite. After finishing her breakfast, she enjoyed a cuddle on my lap as I finished my coffee and read the morning news. After breakfast, she found a cozy place up high to sleep. Sometimes she chooses the couch, and other times, it is a dining room chair or in the middle of the guest bed. In spite of purchasing a hanging cat bed, Ginger prefers to sleep on the antique bed and mattress decorated with a down comforter. She certainly spends a lot of time hiding under or on top of the guest bed, but absolutely no time sleeping in her hanging cat bed!

Ginger loves taking her morning naps, which is fine by me, because I usually go to the gym to work out or take a bike ride along the beach. Our morning routine is set, and when I get home, Ginger is rested and awakens from her nap and signals she is ready for attention and play time. Her preferred play is unrolling the toilet paper rolls in the bathrooms, or pulling Kleenex tissues out of the box, chasing golf balls, ping pong balls, attacking ribbons, and sniffing and licking the cat nip! She loves to be combed and will lay still for me while I comb her. She also enjoys to sit on my lap or on my chest purring loudly as she falls asleep. She needs the connection and views me as her mother. Her favorite perch is the front room window with 3 big windows that look out at a magnolia tree. Ginger can spend hours looking at the birds, lizards, squirrels and geese. She never tires of viewing the outdoors.

Ginger's point of view:

I admit I am famished in the morning, and I cannot wait for my owner to wake up. When she opens her bedroom door, I am so happy to see her because I know the first thing she will do is feed me. I watch from the kitchen floor as she prepares my breakfast on the counter. First, she heats up my wet food and buries it under crunchy dry food with a few treats. I really love having a warm bowl of food for breakfast especially because I don't have to share with other cats like I did before.

After finishing my breakfast, I sit on her lap and cuddle as she watches the news, types on her computer, and sometimes reads to me while sipping coffee from her big blue mug. As her fingers strike the laptop keys, I try to help her and extend both my paws and hit the keys. She swats my paws away repeatedly, and after a while with a full belly, I doze off to sleep.

Later when she gets dressed and leaves the apartment, it is usually for a few hours, so I have the place to myself. I know I am not supposed to jump up onto the kitchen counter, the table or the dressers, but I do it because she cannot scold me. What she doesn't know won't hurt her! My favorite place to hang out is the top of the new bed because it is so comfortable! What cat wouldn't want a mattress that is 14 inches deep and covered in down which is simply perfect for my cat naps? At the foot of the bed is my striped blanket complete with tassels, and I love biting those things! I hang out a lot on or under the bed because it is where I hide my cat nip and toys so she cannot find them. My other favorite place is the front window where the sunlight streams in an warms my body. It is a great place for a nap.

CHAPTER 5:

Hunting time

I discovered as Ginger settled into a routine, that she is quite an expert hunter. In Florida, we have big Palmetto bugs, which are part of the cockroach family. At the young age of three months, which was Ginger's age when I took her home, she caught her first Palmetto bug. I discovered the dead bug on the oriental rug in the living room. I admit I am freaked out finding big cockroach bugs even if they are dead, but I was quick to profusely praise Ginger for her catch. I rewarded her with treats to encourage her to continue hunting for anything that moves, flies or somehow manages to get inside of the apartment!

Over the next few days Ginger continued her insect hunting at night, as cats are nocturnal. She presented a few more bugs over the next several days and continues to chase everything that moves. Recently a small lizard found its' way into the apartment, and the poor thing didn't have a chance with such an experienced hunter. Ginger captured the lizard and again, she was immediately rewarded for her conquest!

Nocturnal: occurring in the night; active at night

Conquest: act or process of conquering or domination

Soon after finding the lizard, I scheduled an exterminator to spray our apartment. They use a spray inside the apartment that is not harmful to humans or pets. With Ginger's expert hunting skills, I won't have to worry because if there is a bug, that she will catch it, because it is what cats do at night!

Ginger doesn't just hunt bugs and lizards, she hunts shiny things as well. A recent example is her attraction to my jewelry that is displayed on the top of my dresser. All of my necklaces and earrings are hung so I can see them. One day something shiny must have caught her eye, because soon after when I was vacuuming the floor something shiny caught my attention. So I bent down for a look and as I retrieved the object, I recognized it was one of my favorite earrings. However, I could not find the mate and I began looking in the second bedroom where Ginger likes to spend her time. I finally located the other earring under the blanket on the bed along with other the earring in the closet that appeared to be shoved underneath the door.

A few days later, I was talking with someone while we were in the second bedroom. She was admiring the artwork on the wall and then she noticed something sparkling on the rug. To my surprise, it was my diamond necklace! So the moral to the story is that Ginger will need to be restricted from my bedroom unless I am home supervising her, otherwise the door will remain shut, or I hide all my jewelry!

Ginger's point of view: Hunting Time

When my owner goes into her bedroom at night, I take a quick cat nap until I know she is sound asleep. Since cats are nocturnal, I spend most of my evening playing and hunting. I love to hunt at night because that's when all the bugs come out from their hiding places, and I want to be ready to pounce on them and play with them. I do this while my owner is sleeping and her door is closed, I love the nighttime because I can catch and play with all the bugs and render them lifeless! At night, I have the run of the apartment all the time because I need to hunt and chase lizards, mosquitoes and Palmetto bugs.

The absolute best part about hunting is the reward I get in the morning when my conquest is discovered! I love it when my owner gets excited, that's why I keep hunting! I need to be more careful though, because the last time I played with and ate a lizard - I got sick. The next morning, I was exhausted, and I was hungry for breakfast, but I was not feeling so great. I ate my breakfast anyway as I usually do, but I couldn't keep the food down. As a result, I vomited so I just hid under the bed and slept all day. You could say that I found out the hard way some lizards have a poisonous coating that can make a cat sick!

I will admit that I love shiny things and there is a plethora on my owner's dresser. When I jump up on top of her dresser, it is like hitting the jackpot! There are hanging shiny necklaces, small glass perfume bottles, and colorful earrings and bracelets. So now you understand why I cannot help myself! I like to hide the jewelry under the rug or the blanket. I got as far one day as hiding an earring in the closet where she could not find it. When she does discover her jewelry, I usually get to play and run while she chases me with the squirt bottle, and I love that game of chase!

CHAPTER 6:

Discipline Time

Little Ginger has been growing as fast as a weed and eating everything in sight. When I sit down to eat, she manages to position herself close to me because she thinks my food is her food. I must make sure when I put her food bowl down that she is busy eating so I have enough time to eat my breakfast and drink my coffee. Otherwise, Ginger is fixated on eating my food. Some days, she cannot get enough and is having a growth spurt.

I have concluded that Ginger needs boundaries and discipline, and she needs this fast. I recently created a plan to address her behavior and filled a handy squirt bottle with water. I carry the squirt bottle with me because the minute I don't have it nearby, Ginger breaks the rules. She thinks it is okay to jump up on the table, my dresser, or kitchen counter. After a few days using the squirt bottle it seemed to be working, but I know she ignores the rules when I leave the apartment.

After a few weeks, it appeared the constant squirting of water was not as successful as I initially thought. Sometimes it did not deter Ginger, and she thought I was playing a game. She was enjoying herself and would display crazy fast running and jumping from room to room and wear herself out. She jumped up quickly and ran out of rooms as I chased behind her trying to squirt her. I concluded I may need to rethink spraying her because water is no longer working.

Ginger is adept at using her litter box, and she has not had any accidents. One day I was cleaning her litter box, and I accidentally left the box of fresh litter on the ground. After hearing an odd sound for a few minutes, I got up to investigate. I thought it was just Ginger being a kitten and playing in the litter box. When I discovered Ginger red handed with her paw in the box of cat litter. It looked as if she was scooping litter out onto the floor. I scolded her and then cleaned up the huge mess, but I learned a valuable lesson. Do not leave the box of clean litter available on the floor with a kitten in the house as they love to play with anything.

Snack Time

Ginger's Perspective: Discipline Time

When I was first introduced to my new home, I caught a big Palmetto bug on my second night. My owner was delighted when she woke up and saw the dead bug laying belly up on the living room carpet. This feat earned me extra treats, and I got combed and then had time cuddling in her lap. From this vantage point, I could watch her type on the computer with the morning news in the background. **Message alert: when I catch more bugs, I get more food and treats!**

I am going to continue my nighttime hunting because it's what I was born to do! Sometimes after I finish my breakfast, I am still hungry and I can smell when my owner starts cooking her breakfast. I just can't help myself so I jump up on her lap to see if I can get a little taste. She redirects me and gives me four treats in the other room. When I finish devouring those heavenly crunchy bites, all that is left to do is settle in for my first cat nap where I can dream of food, lizards or Palmetto bugs.

Okay I admit it, I love to play with just about anything because that is what kittens do. My favorite toys are the ping pong or golf balls because they have a mind of their own and after swatting them, they come to a complete stop. Then all of a sudden the ball begins to roll all over again! I could chase those balls all day!

One day my owner left a box of cat litter on the floor next to my litter box. I noticed a small hole in the box, so I simply put my paw into the box and the litter poured out. I had so much fun watching the granules pile high like a sandcastle. It was like a day playing at the beach! I heard a voice that was louder than usual "No, no, no ... bad do not touch the litter!" It looked like she wanted to play with me because she was kneeling down and swept the litter into a big pile. I just loved the sound of the litter being swept and cleaned up!

CHAPTER 7:

Breaking Bad Habits

Ginger turned five months old and she has become very comfortable in her new surroundings. She has the run of the apartment and there are no limits! She was jumping onto beds, dressers, kitchen counters, and the dining room table. At the time, I didn't give it much thought as she was a kitten. From day one, the fact that she is so darn cute, meant that I did not consistently discipline her.

Early one morning, I noticed Ginger looked dirty, and upon closer inspection I picked her up. It appeared she had soot all over her fur, but especially on her face and paws. It dawned on me that she got into the fireplace! The evidence was all over her face. This meant I would have to use dish soap and warm water to clean off the soot from her fur, and as you know giving cats baths is not something they like. Before the bath, I taped the glass fireplace doors shut to prevent her from getting inside again as I didn't want to give her another bath. I realized kittens can be very curious and need a lot of supervision just like children.

I also noticed that whenever I was preparing a meal, using the cutting board, or simply opening a cabinet, Ginger seemed to be right there - she was comfortable jumping up on the counter to find out firsthand what I was doing. One morning when I was enjoying my coffee, I watched from my chair and out of nowhere, she jumped up onto my lap. She put her nose in my face as if she wanted to get the food that I had inserted into my mouth. The light bulb went off! It was time to put boundaries in place fast for this kitten. But the fact that she was so darn cute meant it was going to be hard.

Ginger liked to scratch my furniture even though there were two scratching pads available for her use to keep her from sharpening her claws on the furniture. I had to keep my new couch covered with a blanket to keep her from scratching it. Of course, I realized scratching is in her nature, so I added a second blanket on the couch, but Ginger still tried to scratch the exposed sides and back of the couch.

I bought a natural spray product designed to deter cats from scratching. However, I still caught her scratching my couch and chair, so I decided to purchase double stick tape and wrapped the tape around the couch. When I came home that day, I witnessed Ginger actually pulling the tape off the couch with her teeth, so that didn't work! A few days later I caught Ginger on top of my dresser when I heard something crash to the ground and break.

I ran into the bedroom and found evidence of a perfume bottle shattered on the floor. There was compelling evidence for some new rules to be created. I got out a spray bottle and filled it with water. Each time Ginger would jump up onto the counter, dresser, table or my red leather chair, I would warn her using a stern voice. Then I would place her back on the ground, and if she immediately jumped back up. she would be sprayed with a water bottle.

The first time I sprayed Ginger with water, she froze in her tracks. However, she continued to require reminders to stay off the counters, table and couch. This meant more sprays from the water bottle - but it appeared she was catching on to the new discipline rules. After about one week, Ginger's behavior vastly improved, and although she still exhibited the need to scratch and jump, I added two more scratching posts for her use and continued with positive praise when she did follow the rules.

Do you know why do cats scratch?

- Helps reduce energy/stress

- Cats mark their territory: did you know they have glands on their paws?

- Cats enjoy a good stretch and do this when scratching

The solution to scratching is to redirect behavior:

- Find good alternative scratching posts

- Use aluminum foil and cover the area

- Use double sided sticky tape or paws

- Use natural repellant spray

Ginger's Perspective: Breaking Bad Habits

I thought this new home was so great because I got to do whatever I wanted, and my owner encouraged me. Then one day all of a sudden, she began scolding me using a loud and low voice. She told me "NO" all the time which confused me because all the rules changed. Now I had to stay on the floor or underneath the table on the chair cushions. She brought out a squirt bottle and started spraying me. She caught me off guard and I got soaked when I jumped up on the counter looking for snacks. But now when I heard her voice and saw her pointing a blue bottle in my direction, I paused and that is when she yelled a second time and sprayed me. I guess the rules were really changing and she wasn't playing with me. Well, at least when she goes to sleep I can resume my behavior.

A few hours later I was sharpening my claws on the back of the couch, and out of nowhere I got blasted with about five squirts from the bottle. I was surprised and froze again, but I got the message because she was yelling at me repeatedly: "NO, NO, NO bad kitty." I darted off to her bedroom until she calmed down. In her bedroom, I decided to jump up on top of her dresser where there is a lot of cool stuff. I found some glass perfume bottles with little droppers and swatted them, but it went crashing to the floor. That's when my owner came running, and I could tell she wasn't happy. She was yelling, "NO, NO, NO, bad kitty." I just looked at her and for a second, I thought something is going on, and that's when I got soaked again!

I know she kept the couch covered in tape and blankets so I wouldn't scratch it, but I am a kitten, and that's what kittens do! I intensely disliked the double stick tape because when I put my paws on the couch, the tape stuck to them. I didn't like the feeling because I couldn't scratch. I decided to use my teeth to bite the tape off. Wouldn't you know she caught me in the act! You probably know what happened next. That's right, I got squirted and this time I was drenched. I hid out underneath her bed until she calmed down and put the squirt bottle away. While I was under the bed, I had time to think about all the changes I was facing. I could no longer do what I pleased, all the rules changed overnight. I wondered, "What else did she have in store for me?" In the meantime, I got used to this game of chase, and I actually enjoyed getting squirted. It was fun, so I would jump up and do something wrong, and on demand she would come running with the squirt bottle. This was great exercise but it certainly wore me out.

Reasons against declawing kittens and cats:

- They can develop arthritis in hands and feet

- When claws are removed, the cat may feel threatened and act out of fear and may be more likely to bite

- They may not be able to use the litter box appropriately as declawing procedures cause pain

<u>*Declawing: also known as nail removal)</u>

CHAPTER 8:

Discovering the outdoors

I thought about what else I could do to help Ginger release her energy as she was running around the house like a psycho kitty. I purchased a harness to take Ginger outside, and upon the first attempt, she wasn't quite sure how to behave on a leash. She sat there and I coaxed her, but in reality she did not know what she was supposed to do, I began taking her out and put the harness on her. In case she ever got out of the house, she would know where the front door is located and come home. We started out slowly going for just a few minutes each day. At first, we sat outside on the patio chair with Ginger in my lap, and a few days later she advanced to laying underneath the chair where she could watch the small lizards dart in and out of the grasses and plants.

It didn't take long for Ginger to enjoy going out for fresh air and waiting near the door. Initially, she would lay down when I put her harness on. She preferred to hide in the natural grasses for cover in case birds, dogs or geese got too close as she was intimidated by their size. A few weeks later when renovation on the outside of the apartment building began; the noise and workers have been a deterrent for Ginger, and she hesitated going outside. Once I open the door, she peeks to make sure the coast is clear, but there were a few times she couldn't be coaxed to venture out.

However, in the evening when the workers leave and it was quiet, she quickly overcame her hesitancy and began waiting at the door for me to take her out. When I take out her harness and leash, she lays down and allows me to put it on. This indicates she is ready to begin her exploration for lizards and bugs especially after the traffic and noise outside the apartment subsides. Only then does Ginger relax and lay down on the grass taking in the fresh air and view of the lake, watching the turtles sun themselves, and observes the numerous birds that dart across the sky from tree to tree. She loves lying in the grass watching everything, as long as, no geese, dogs or people are around to spook her.

Leash training begins

Ginger's Perspective: Going Outside

At first I admit, I didn't like going outside the apartment because I had to put on a harness that she made me wear. I was happy inside because I was safe, and I had the run of the house except for the counters, table and couch. I didn't know what to do the first time she took me outside, so she kind of dragged me or picked me up and carried me for the first week or so. I admit I become easily scared by movement, noise or even the wind, because in my life, I haven't spent much time outside.

But after a few weeks practicing going outside with the harness on, I began to appreciate the fresh air, sunshine, and the beauty of the nearby lake and landscaping surrounding the apartment. For several days we ventured outside, and then I realized there was a lot to see and do. I could look for bugs and lizards, and I slowly overcame my fears because my owner stays with me while I am outside. So now when I go out, I can catch lizards, and when I caught my first lizard, I was happy because it's what I do and there are tons of them.

I decided that going outside would allow me to enjoy the fresh air and I began to look forward to going outside. Also, I am closer to the lizards that hide outside in the native grasses and they are everywhere. I am all in with taking a stroll outside for an adventure. About 15 yards from the front door is a lake, and there is so much to see and listen for on any given day. There are a couple families of geese, and you can hear them because they can be loud and annoying, and sometimes they fly right over me. I think when they do that they are protecting their babies.

Also, the black birds are annoying and talk non-stop, and it sounds like all they say when I am outside is "Un Uh" repeatedly. They circle the sky looking for prey and communicate to the other birds whenever they see something. I like the turtles second best because they are slow moving and sit for hours sunning themselves on the grassy bank, just like me. Some animals are bigger than me, and I don't want to be their dinner! I keep my body as low to the ground as possible to camouflage myself underneath the porch stairs, the palm tree or the foliage next to the building.

CHAPTER 9:

No longer a kitten

It's hard to believe that almost five months have passed and Ginger has doubled in size and she is thriving. She is not a huge cat. In fact she has small paws, but she is growing longer and has put on a few pounds. She appreciates a schedule which includes bedtime at 10:30 pm, and wakeup time up at 6:30 am for breakfast. After eating, it is always play time, and she loves getting treats and will do just about anything to get one. She runs around the house, into the tub and sinks, waiting for me to chase her and get close enough to squirt her.

That discipline still needs work as she enjoys playing and having me chase her and squirt her. I think she views me as both mother and a playmate. Ultimately, we have a great schedule as now Ginger can be trusted to be home alone. I am confident nothing will be broken when I get home. When I leave the house, she usually sleeps the entire time. In the morning, she chooses my bed for her first nap. This makes sense because the bed is always made and there is a fluffy down comforter on it. In the afternoon Ginger sleeps underneath the dining room table on one of the chairs. Later she jumps up onto my lap and tries to lick my hands and distract me when I am typing on my laptop. Her favorite thing to do is reach out and strike the keys herself and she appears to be right handed.

Little Ginger provides entertainment on a daily basis and makes everything better and continues to put a smile on my face. Her independent streak is countered with a need for love and connection. She loves our cuddles, play time, treats, grooming, daily walks, and squirt bottle exchange. She has brought so much happiness to my life that it is hard to express it with words. I just know that she is a keeper, and my life is better since I rescued her.

Ginger in bloom

Ginger's perspective:

Don't get me wrong, I love everything about my new home and my owner, but as a kitten I require a lot of sleep. I am almost five months young and I have doubled in size. I noticed when I tried to jump up onto a dining room chair, I hit my head on the tabletop, and that never happened before. I am going to have to remember to slow down and make sure I fit. When my owner feeds me first thing in the morning, I eat fast and then play a bit. I love to run and jump and chase golf balls and ping pong balls. So before I chill out and take my first nap, I usually pick the quietest place, and each day that changes because there has been a lot of construction on our apartment. My first choice is either her bed, or under the bed in the second bedroom, and if needed on the sink in the bathroom because it is nice an cool and cozy. We don't have any sun coming through some windows, but temporarily that is okay, because I am a growing cat who needs a lot of beauty sleep.

My owner usually leaves each morning around 9 am for a few hours, so it is ideal sleeping time for me. If she does come back after an hour or two, she does her thing and either makes breakfast, reads, types or watches the news. She usually lets me sleep, but if she does start bothering me, I remove myself and hide under the middle of the bed where she can't reach me and pick me up or hug and kiss on me. Most days I can sleep for several hours. I may wake up to use the litter box or get a drink of water, but then it's off to dreamland again for my second nap. So that pretty much sums up my day: eat, sleep and repeat!

CHAPTER 10:

Curiosity gets the best of Ginger

Ginger is very curious and one day managed to get out of the house through an opening in the kitchen between the baseboard underneath the dishwasher and kitchen sink. When I got up in the morning and I was feeding her, I noticed she looked dirty, and dirt is easy to spot on a white cat. When I picked her up and closely examined her, the dirt was all over especially on her paws, face and belly. After cleaning her up and feeding her breakfast, I decided to investigate if and where she may have gotten out. As the fireplace was taped shut, I went outside and looked for access points where she could have gotten out (remember the apartment is still under renovation.) When I spotted the new small round hole outside the kitchen wall, I immediately knew where she made her exit to the outside world. I was concerned because like a baby, anything could happen to her while she was unsupervised.

After cleaning her up, I gave her breakfast. She ate all of her breakfast and then began her usual routine of running around, begging for treats and napping. I went about my day and took a long bike ride. I arrived home about two hours later to eat a big breakfast and then check in on her. She was fine because I blocked her access point in the kitchen. She wasn't happy about it and repeatedly tried to go back to it. This was her hiding place and newest access to the outside world. I couldn't risk her getting out again, after all anything could happen to her.

The rest of the day was typical. I did some laundry and I waited for a friend to come over and help me move a piece of furniture. After we did so, I put the blanket we had used to move the furniture into the washer. Later after the furniture was in place, I put the blanket into the dryer and sat down to relax and watch a little tv. That was when I saw Ginger in the hallway, and I called her, but she didn't respond. Rather she went into the second bedroom, and at that point, I noticed the dryer door was open. I thought that was odd but maybe the bulk of the blanket caused it to open.

I got up and closed the dryer door and turned it back on. I looked for Ginger and found her in the second bedroom under the bed. I brought her a treat, but she didn't move. I suspected something was wrong because she always comes right to me for a treat. I crawled under the bed and pulled Ginger out. I was alarmed when I saw blood and feces all over her paws and fur. I looked in the hallway between the dryer and bedroom and noticed what looked like blood on the floor. I took Ginger into the bathroom and wrapped her in a towel to cover her back legs so she couldn't kick me. After rinsing her front paws with cool water and quickly Examining her for cuts, I was relieved to see she did not have any. I wiped her off, and it was then that I realized Ginger had an accident and wasn't able to make it to the litter box.

It was at that moment that I remembered she had gotten out earlier in the day. She was fighting me as I washed her fur and wrapped her in a towel. She got away and went back under the bed to hide. I had to pull her out again, and that is when I smelled feces. She was obviously very sick and unable to clean herself. Never before did she have an accident, so I used disinfectant wipes to clean and dry her off. I realized she must have caught and ate a lizard because she was so sick. The toxic covering of a lizards' skin can affect cats and render them extremely sick. When she was clean, I left her to rest and periodically checked on her and gave her some water.

Ginger refused to eat any food or water until the next day when she began feeling better. She was able to eat a little food and drink from her water fountain. She did let me comb her and inspect her, and she laid on my lap and took a nice long nap. She stayed very close to me, but this was different from the first time she caught a lizard and got sick. Kittens are similar to newborns, they cannot communicate their needs, nor tell us when they are sick. They are not aware that animals such as lizards, can hurt them.

So kittens need to be carefully monitored as it is in their nature to hide any illness. Cats are born predators – it is in their DNA to hunt and chase moving things, but lizards can be toxic to cats. The first three signs to look for if your cat has caught or eaten a lizard: loss of appetite, lethargy, and unusual bathroom patterns. Well, that described Ginger's behavior perfectly, but the whole event was scary. I covered the newest hole with towels and weights which she cannot move. I comforted her and gave her space to sleep, but I also kept a close watch.

Ginger's point of view

I noticed when I went under the counter that a new hole appeared, and it was as if my wishes had come true. I ventured outside for a little bit, but when I got back inside my owner noticed the new hole. I guess the tip off was the fact that I was covered in dirt and she spotted me right away. She scooped me up and washed me off using a sponge with a little bit of soap. I guess she saw my dirty paws, my dirty face and I got caught - but it was worth a few minutes of freedom.

When I snuck out using the new access hole, I hunted for and caught my second lizard. When the lizard stopped moving, I had him for lunch. Soon after my escapade, I returned to the kitchen as she was calling my name. I knew if I responded she would give me a few treats, so I graced her with my presence and meowed loudly for attention. After I ate the treats, I noticed she blocked my access point to the outside world, but what could I do? She was not listening to my complaints or meows. She wasn't budging and her weights stayed at the entrance to my hole.

Later my stomach began to hurt, so I went and hid under the bed to sleep where no one can reach me. After my nap, I woke up feeling very nauseous…I tried to make it to the litter box, but it was no use and I vomited in the hallway. I noticed my favorite blanket was in the dryer and the door was open, so I went in there to hide. I felt really sick, and I had an accident because I couldn't make it to the litter box.

Of course, my owner had just come home and saw me, and when she called me to come to her, I was too sick to do so. I had no energy and just wanted to hide under the bed. The lizard I ate had made me so sick, I could hardly walk. A few minutes later she tried to entice me out from under the bed with some treats, but to be honest, I was too sick to care. That was when she grabbed me by the fur and pulled me out. She knew something was very wrong, I mean I stunk, I had no energy, and I felt terrible.

CHAPTER 11:

Surviving and thriving

So by now, you can tell that Ginger is an independent and overly curious cat with a tendency to get into and out of trouble around our apartment. She is very intelligent and filled with energy. At the same time, Ginger displays love and charms everyone who encounters her. Most people say she is a beautiful cat, and she manages to bring a smile to my face several times a day even when she is naughty. I attribute her energy and curiosity to her age and the fact that she is still teething and learning.

We continue our evening walks with her on harness near the lake. She appears much more relaxed, and I have no doubt that she will adjust to the sounds of the outside and thrive in the years to come. We sit out on the patio each day and she gets combed so the hair isn't inside the apartment. We still cuddle and I am thinking that our next adventure will be seeing how Ginger would do on a bike ride.

I could harness her and find a comfortable bike carrier with a mesh covering and a leash to provide a view and an incentive not to jump out. Right now she can go on short bike rides and get some fresh air. This means, she would be less than two feet from me allowing me to keep my eyes on her and ensure her safety. She can take in the sights and sounds, but will need to be restrained so she doesn't try to jump out of the basket. Who knows, I may even have to get her some sunglasses and a visor because it is sunny in Florida. There is so much to see, but safety is first. Look out for Super Kitty on a bike near you!

After writing this book, I thought I had adopted Ginger, but really she adopted me. She has turned out to be a great companion and a ton of fun. Welcome to the family!

Ginger's point of view:

I love new adventures, and I am all for whatever gets me out of the house and into the fresh air. There is so much to see and do outside, but one thing I will not do is eat any more lizards or frogs. I have learned my lesson and the memories are ingrained in my brain. I would love to go on a bike ride because almost every day my owner wheels her bike out of the house. She is gone about two hours, and I have no idea where she goes or what she's doing. It makes me kind of jealous because I have to stay home, and there is nothing going on, so I just sleep the mornings away.

However, I have distant memories of my car ride from the CC to my new home. So I would love the opportunity to get out for another car or even a bike ride. I remember how much there was to take in: trees, birds, people, cars, and bikes. A bike ride sure beats sleeping my mornings away, and I would get to spend more time with my owner. I have a feeling there are many more adventures in my future, and I look forward to getting out and enjoying the sights and sounds of the city.

Websites for kids:

1. Humane Society

   8684 Beach Boulevard,

   Jacksonville, FL

   Jaxhumane.org

   > Click on adopt

   > Select dog or cat photos

2. Caffeinated Cat

   331 1st Avenue North

   904-853-5154

   https://www.facebook.com/thecaffeinatedcatjax

Definitions:

Nocturnal: of, relating to, or occurring in the night

Declaw: to remove the claws of (an animal such as a cat) surgically